The River Wharfe at Bolton Bridge (Stage 1)

THE DALES WAY

The Dales Way is a scenic 79 mile route between Ilkley and Bowness-on-Windermere, linking the Yorkshire Dales with the Lake District. Well served for accommodation and facilities and with easy walking on riverside paths, the Dales Way is one of the gentlest multi-day walks in Britain, and therefore an ideal introduction to long-distance walking. It can be comfortably completed in 6–8 days.

Contents and using this guide

This booklet of Ordnance Survey 1:25,000 Explorer maps has been designed for convenient use on the trail and includes:

- a key to map pages (pages 2–3) showing where to find the maps for each stage
- the full and up-to-date line of the Dales Way, designed for use in both directions
- an extract from the OS Explorer map legend (pages 44–46)

The companion guidebook, *The Dales Way*, describes the full route in both directions alongside all you need to plan a successful trip.

© Cicerone Press 2021
ISBN-13: 978 1 78631 094 1
Photos © Terry Marsh 2021

© Crown copyright 2021
OS PU100012932

THE DALES WAY

Wharfedale
Stage 1   Ilkley to Burnsall 5
Stage 2   Burnsall to Buckden 10

Langstrothdale and Dentdale
Stage 3   Buckden to Cowgill (Lea Yeat) 16
Stage 3A The Watershed Alternative 27
Stage 4   Cowgill (Lea Yeat) to Millthrop (Sedbergh) 27

Lonsdale and the Lakeland Fringe
Stage 5   Millthrop (Sedbergh) to Staveley 33

Into Lakeland
Stage 6   Staveley to Bowness-on-Windermere 40

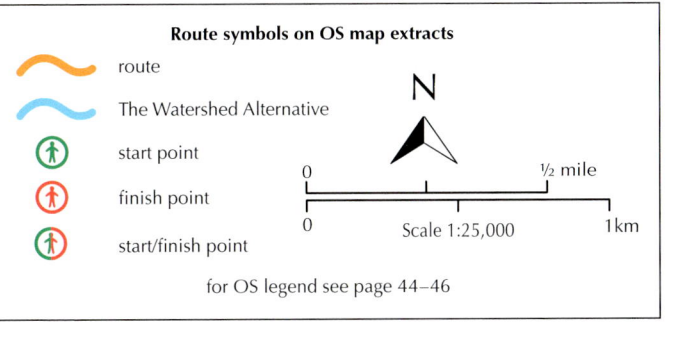

Route symbols on OS map extracts

- ～ route
- ～ The Watershed Alternative
- 🚶 start point
- 🚶 finish point
- 🚶 start/finish point

N

0 — ½ mile
0 — Scale 1:25,000 — 1km

for OS legend see page 44–46

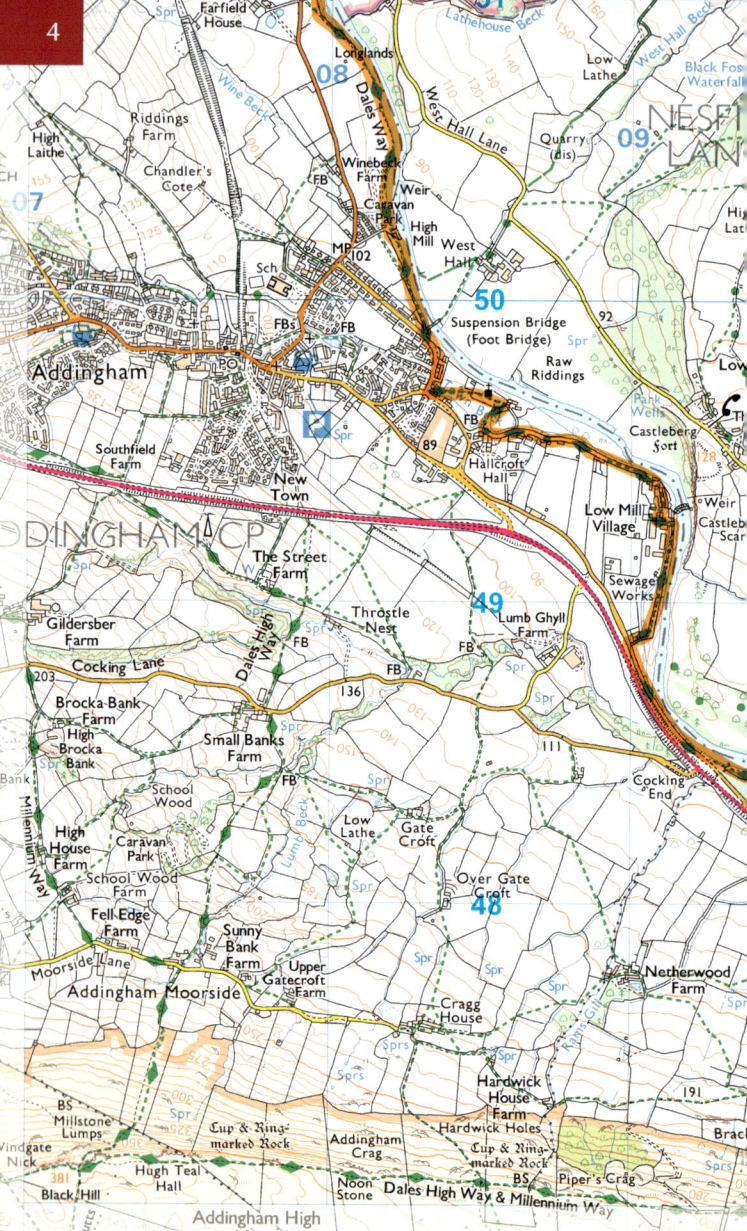

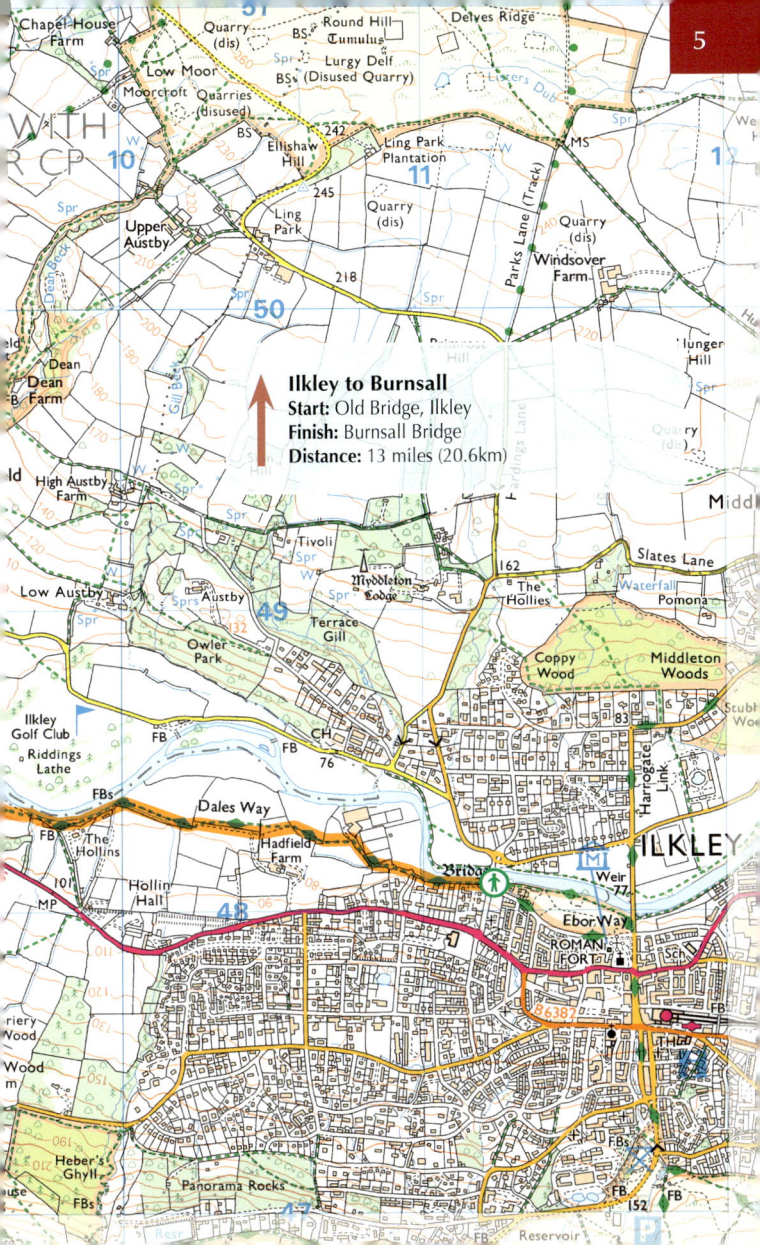

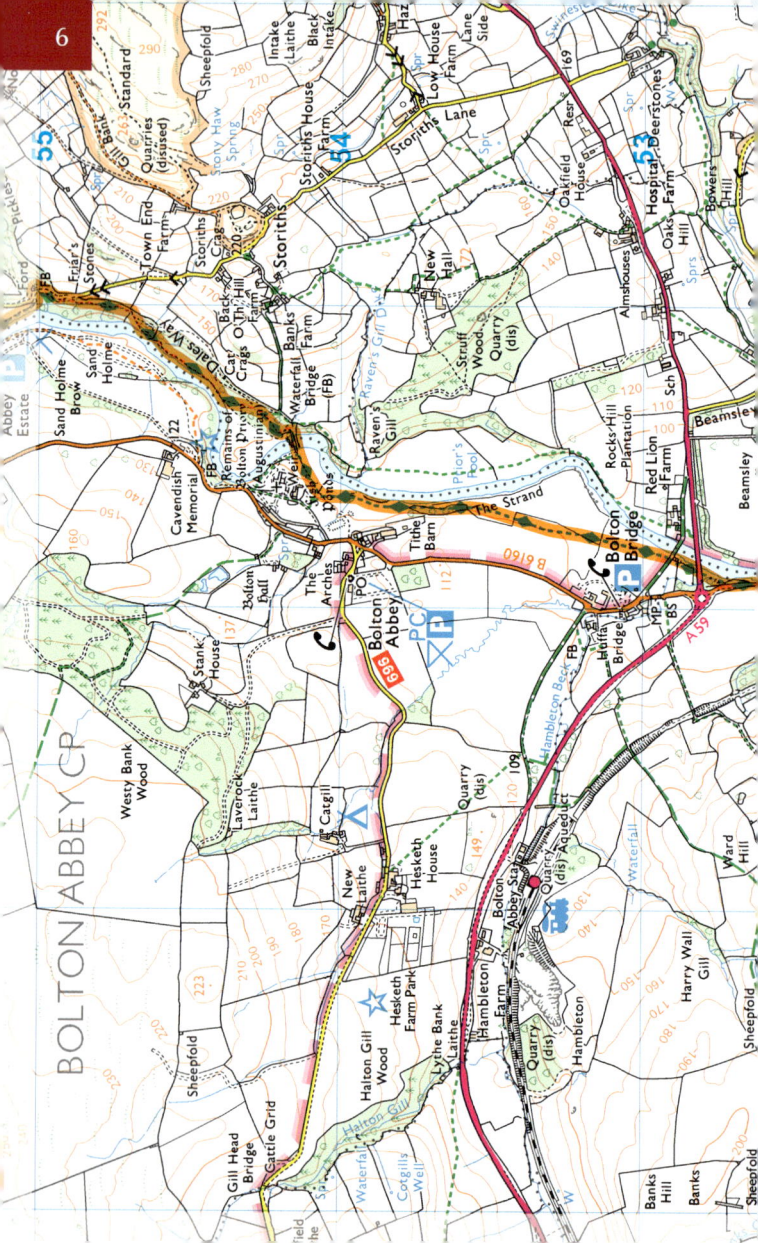

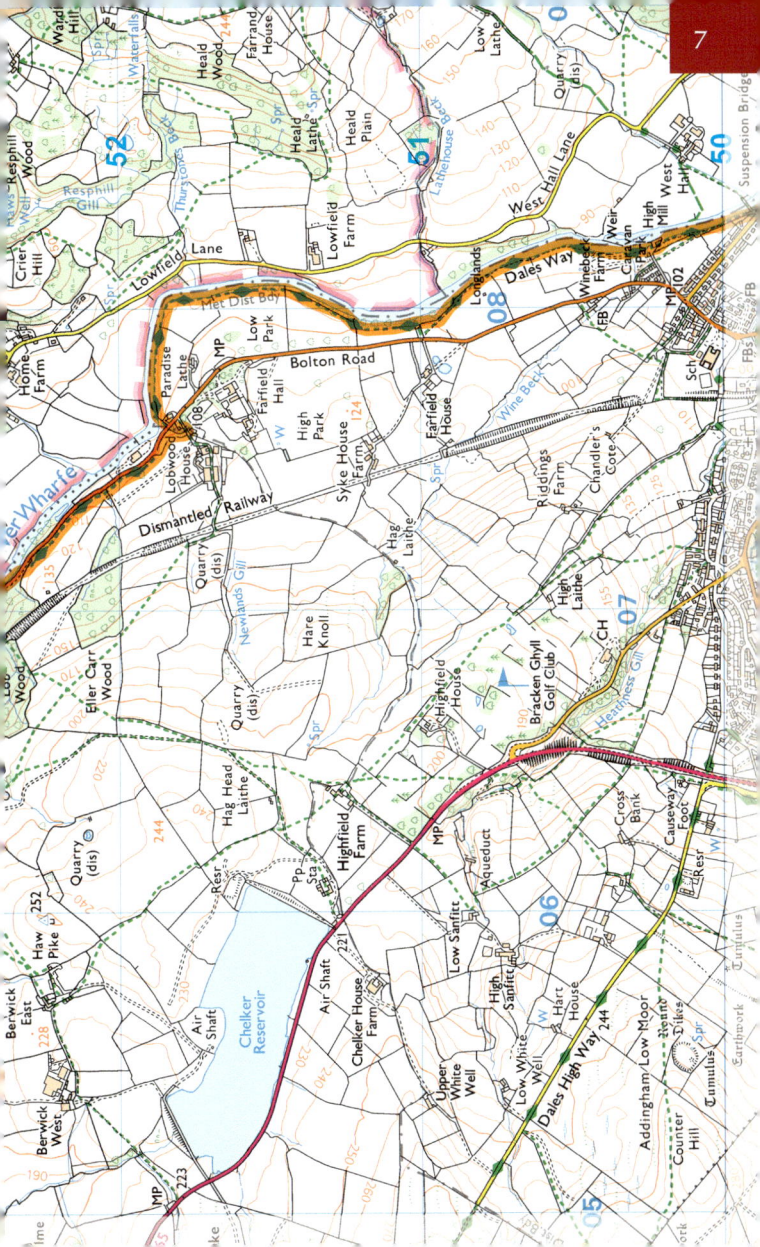

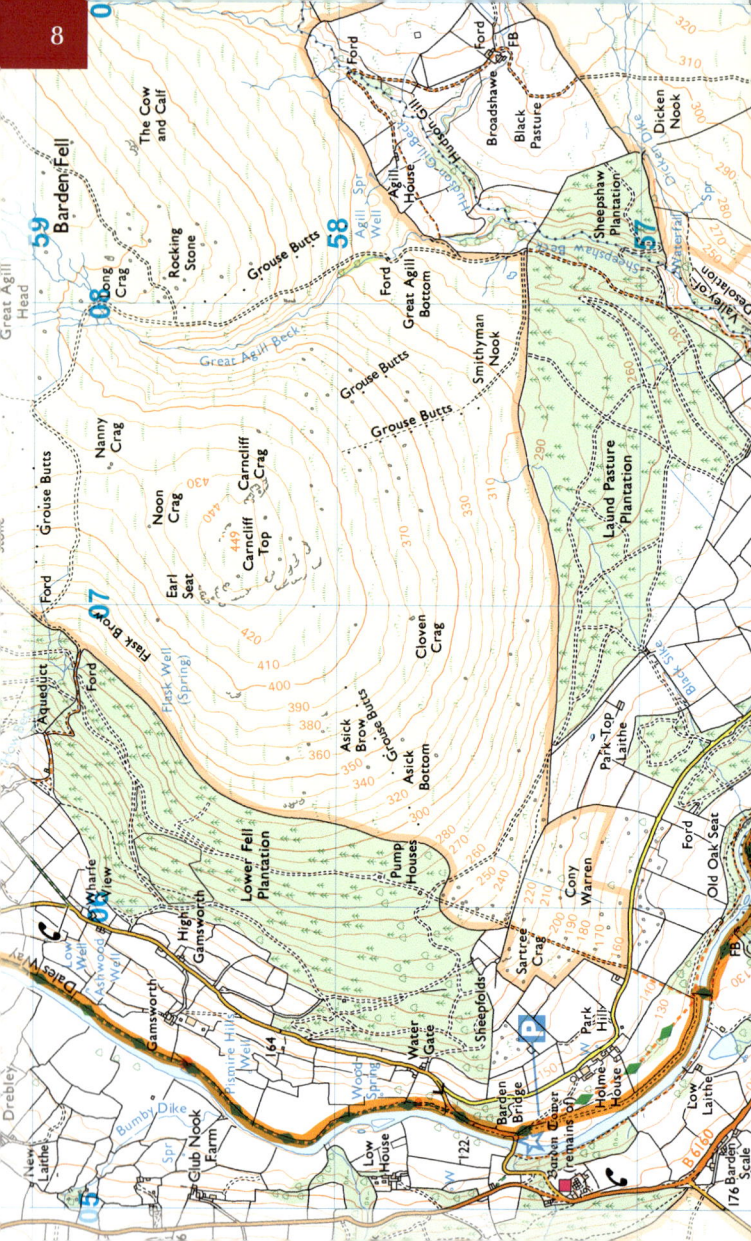

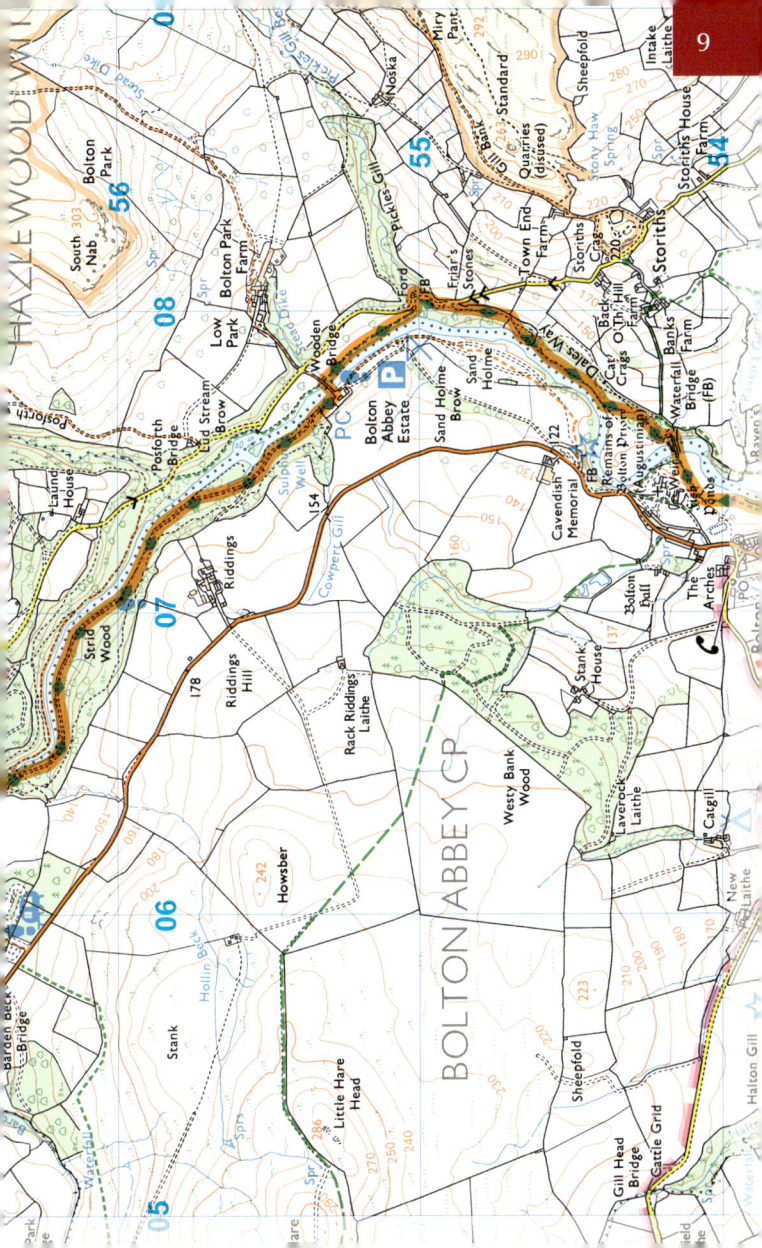

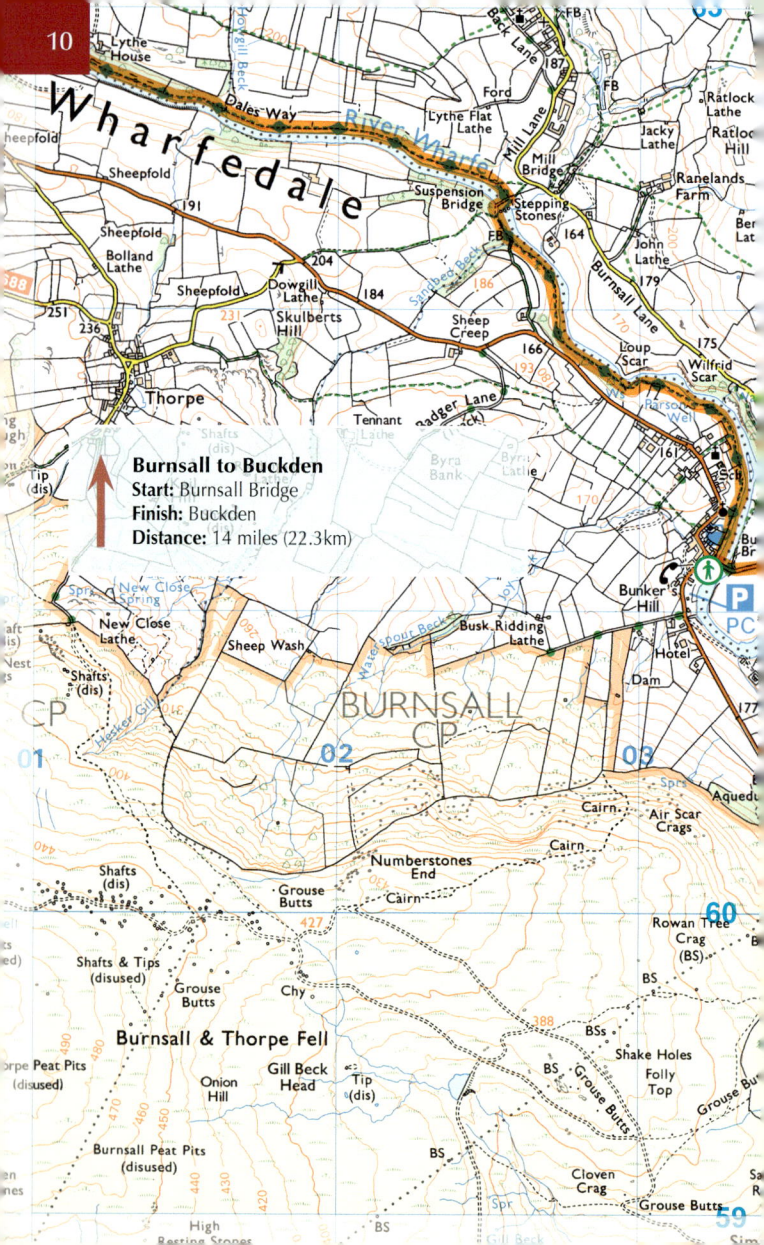

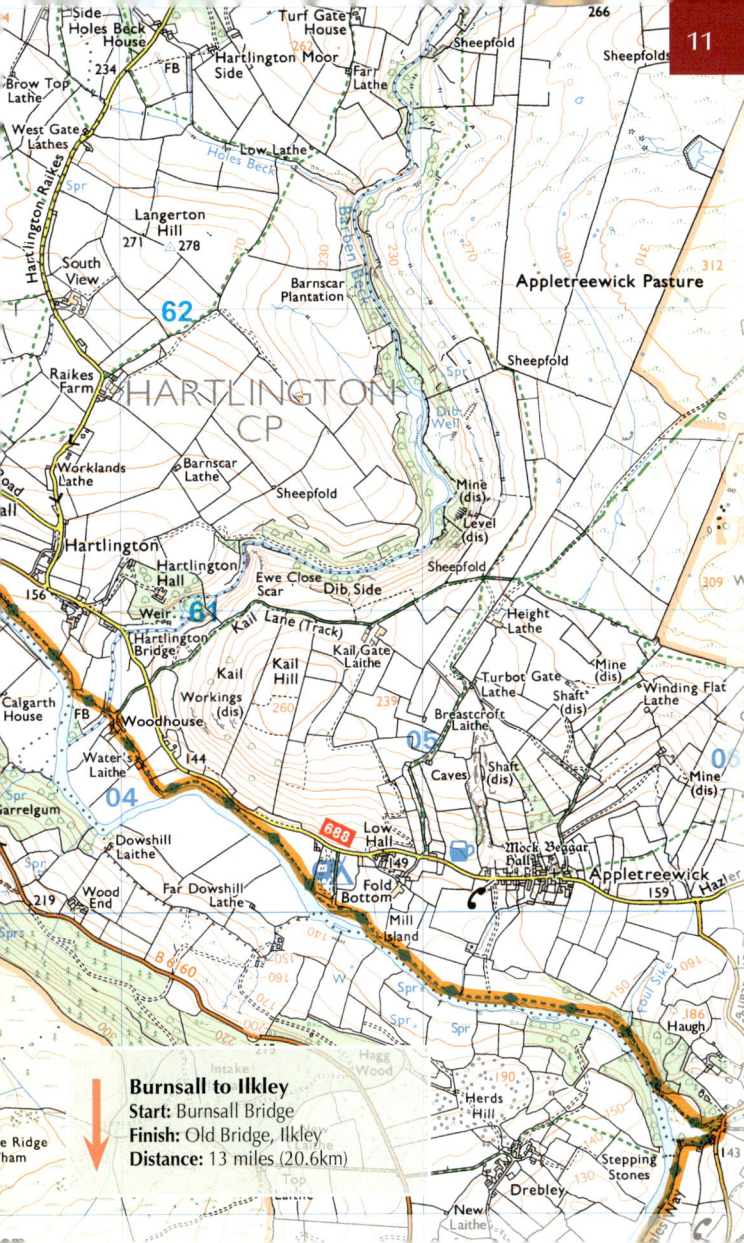

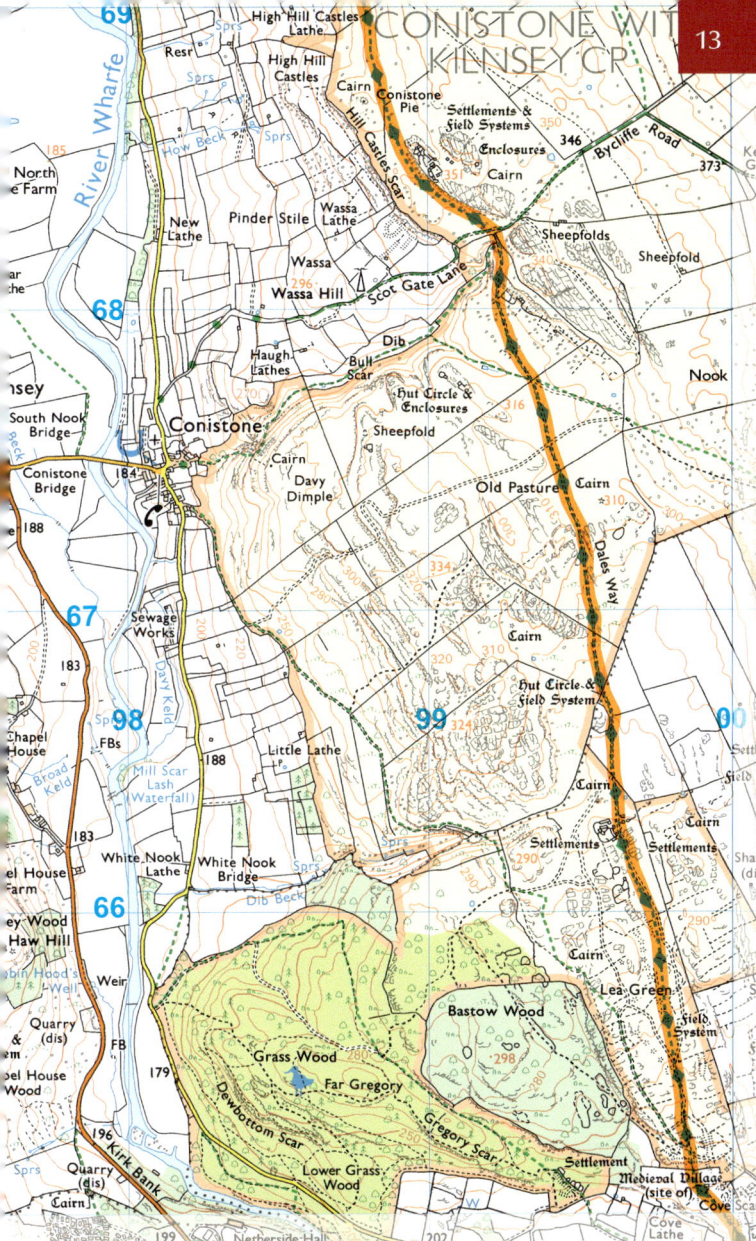

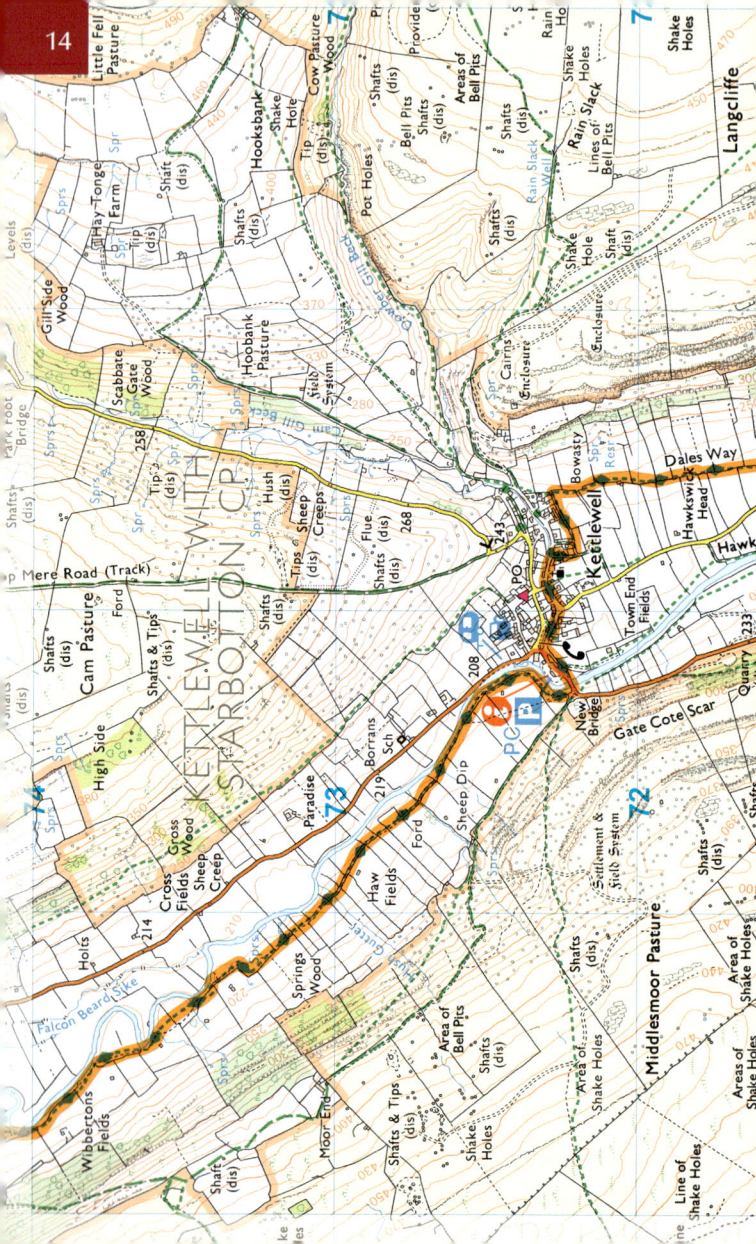

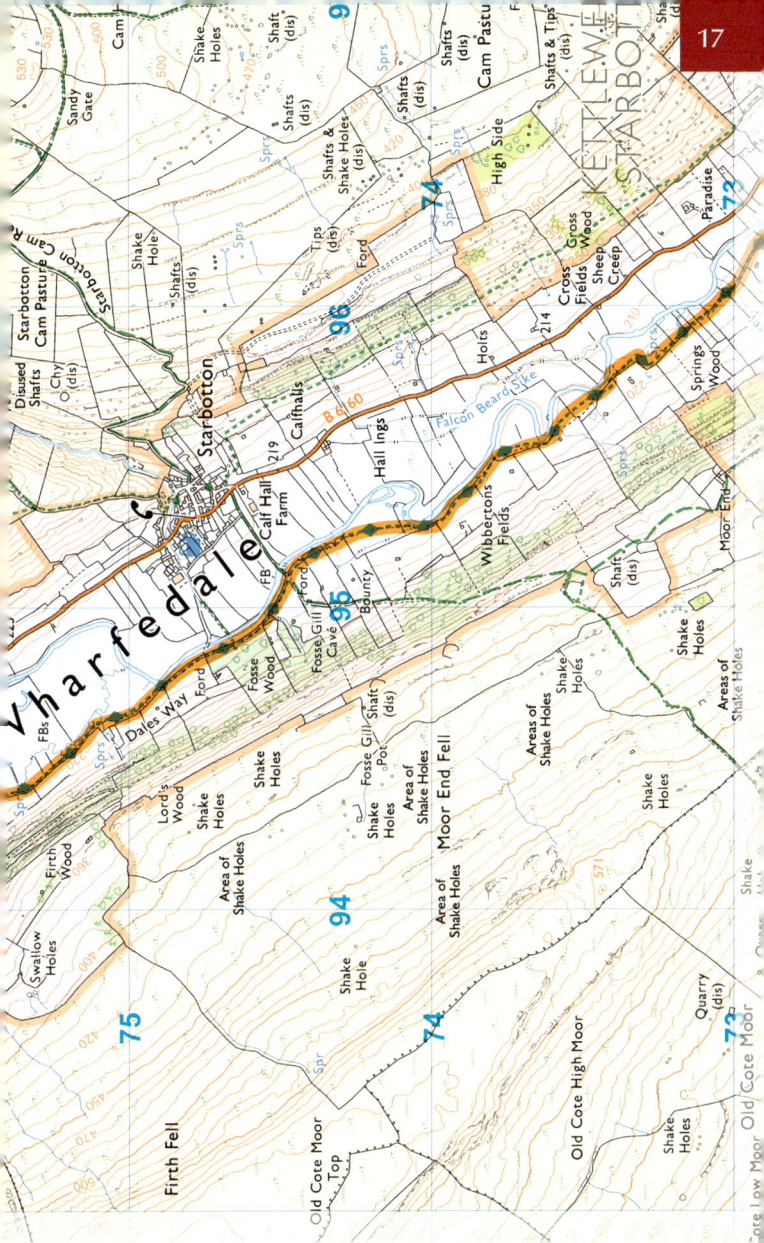

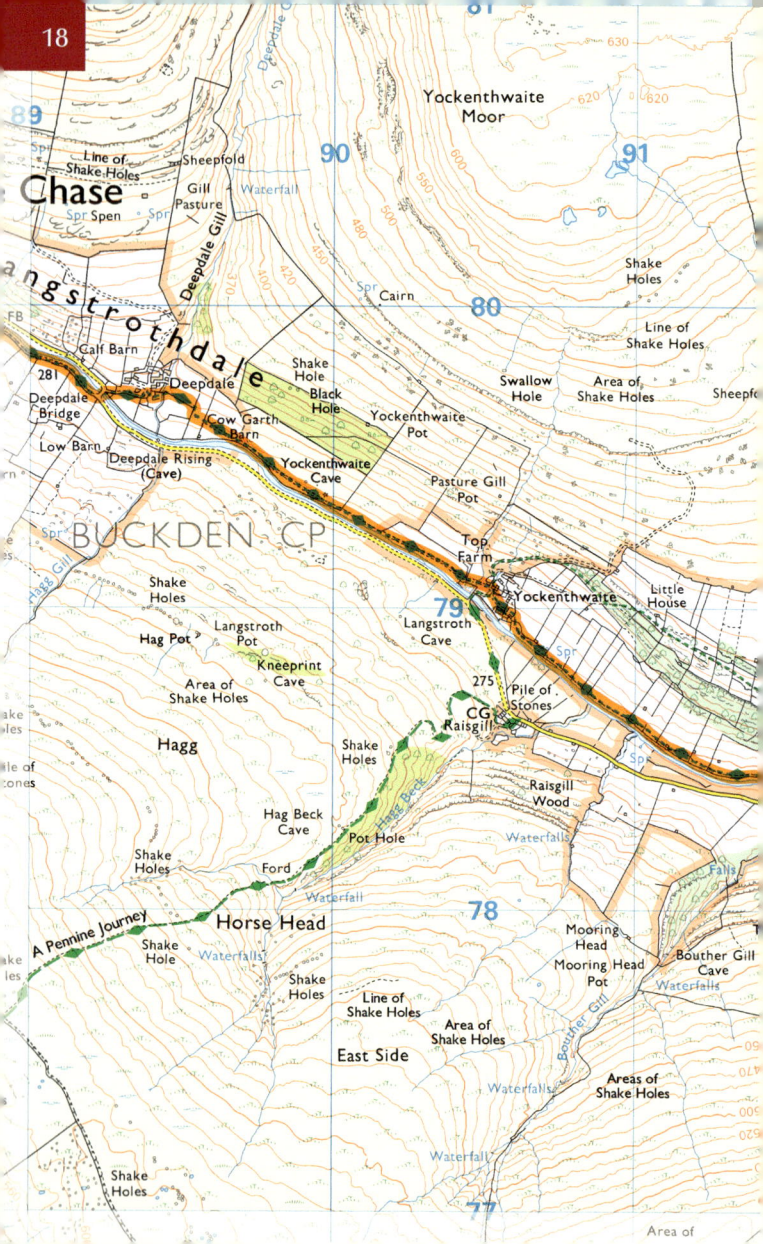

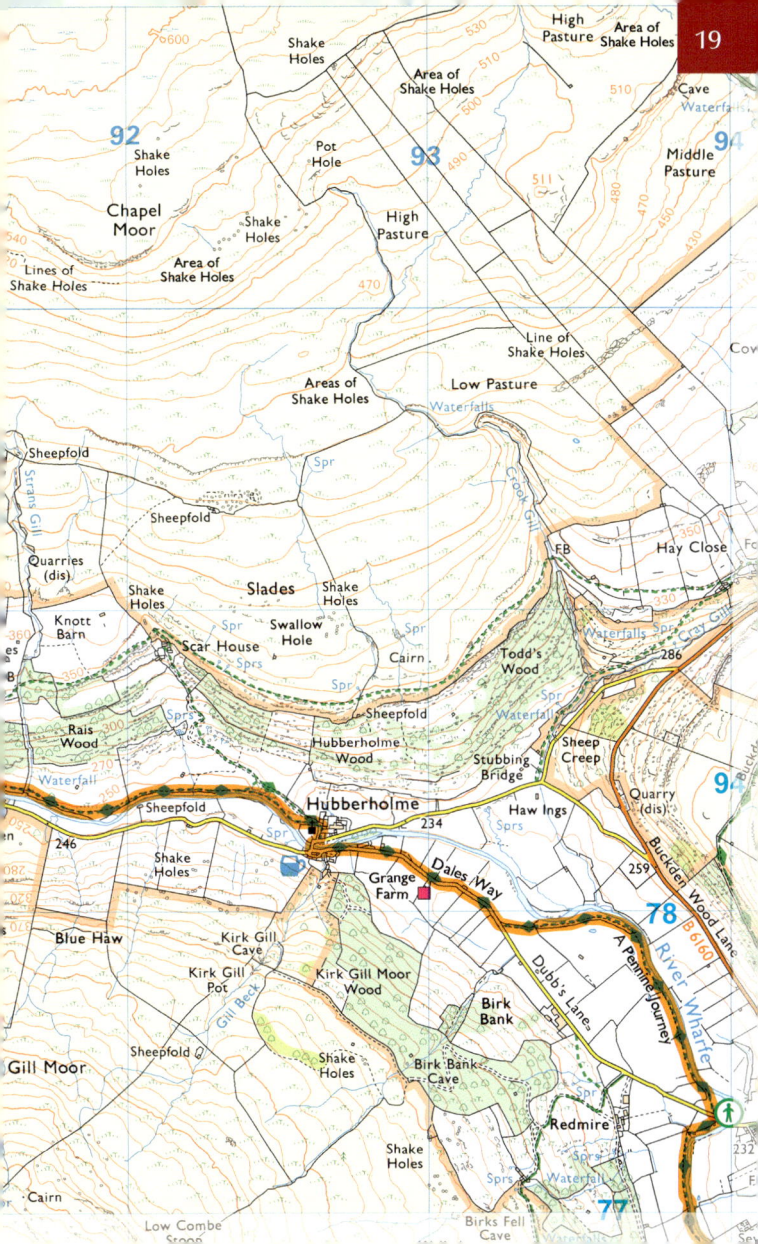

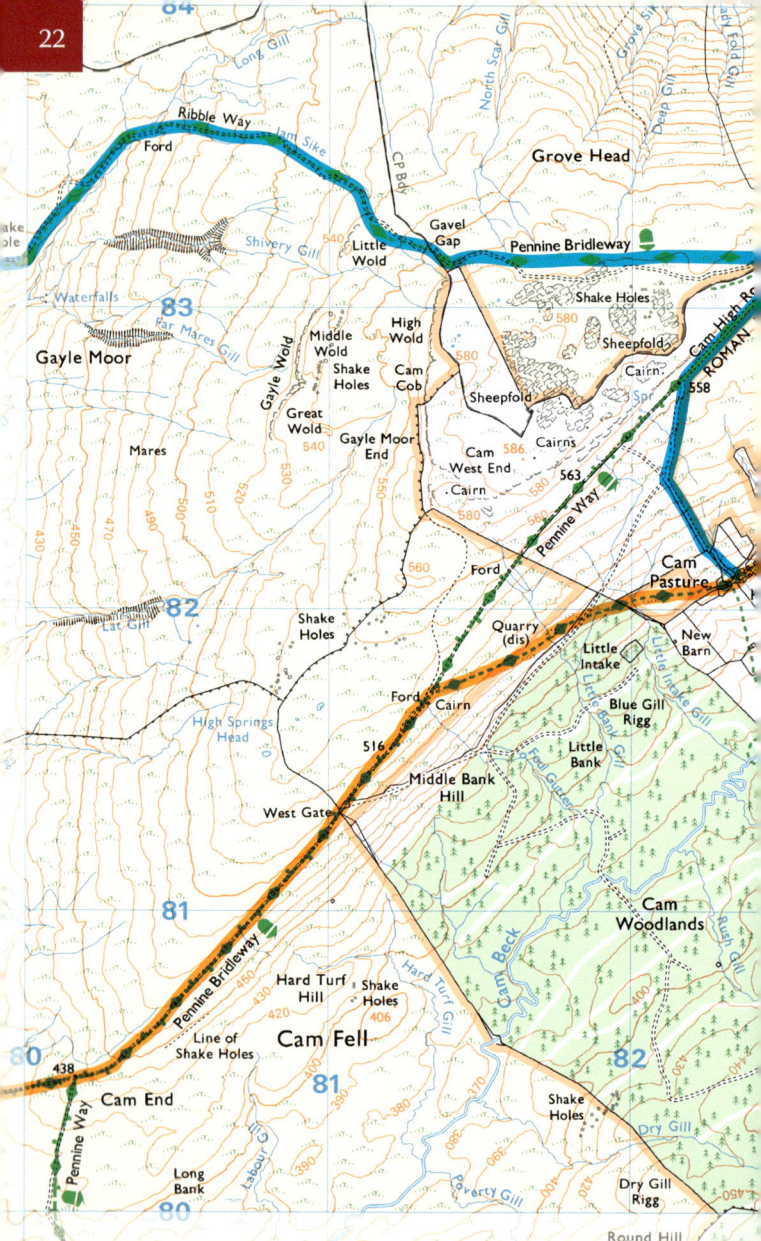

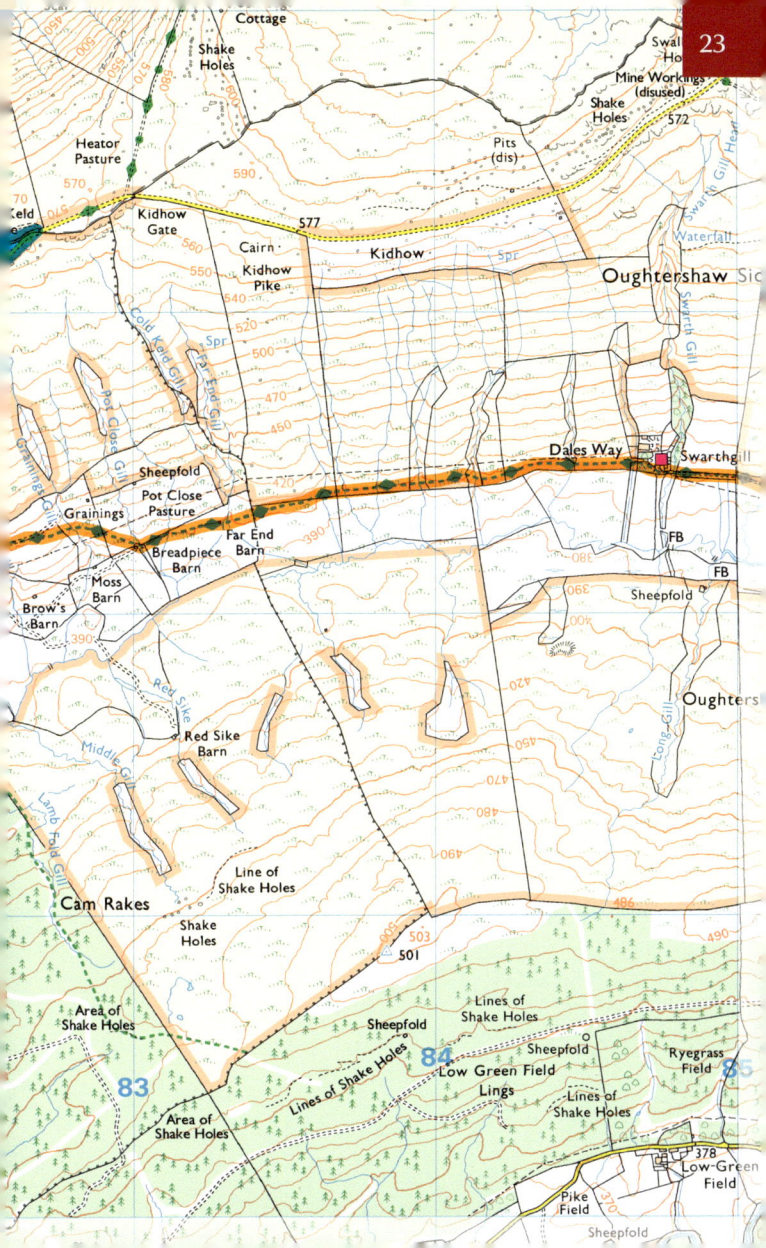

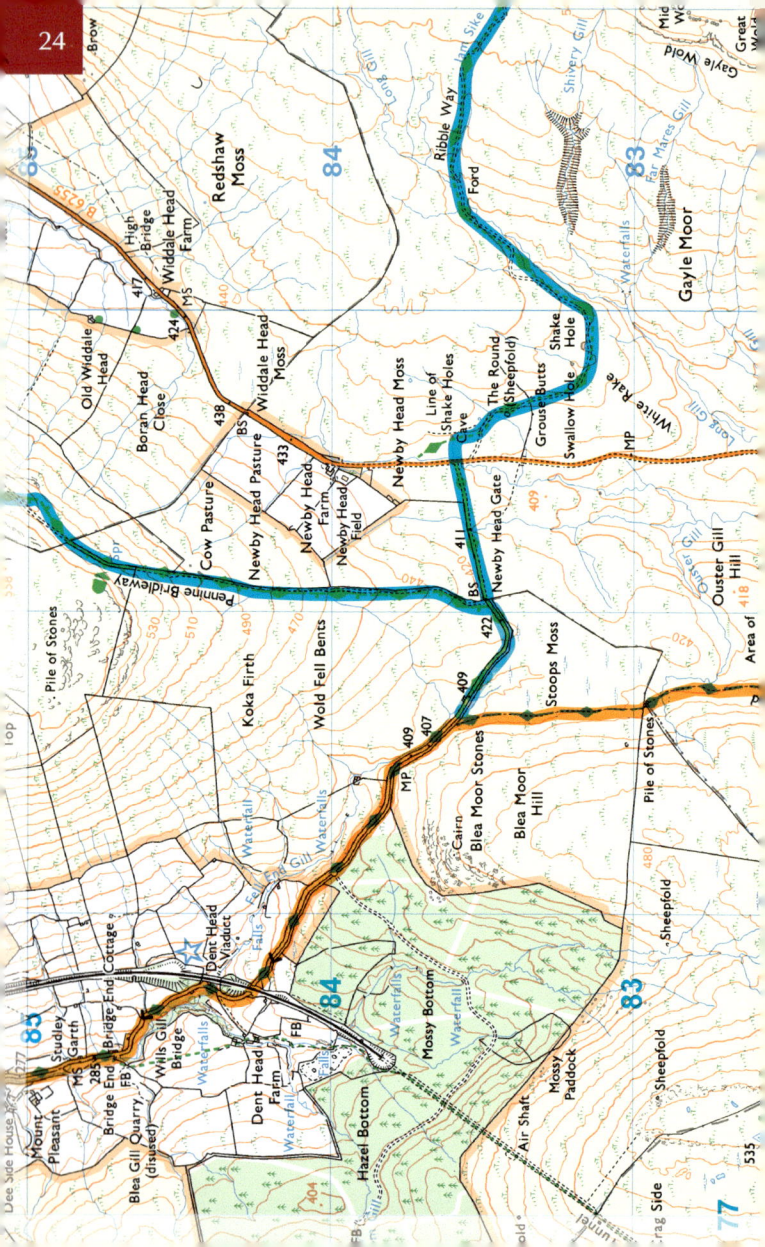

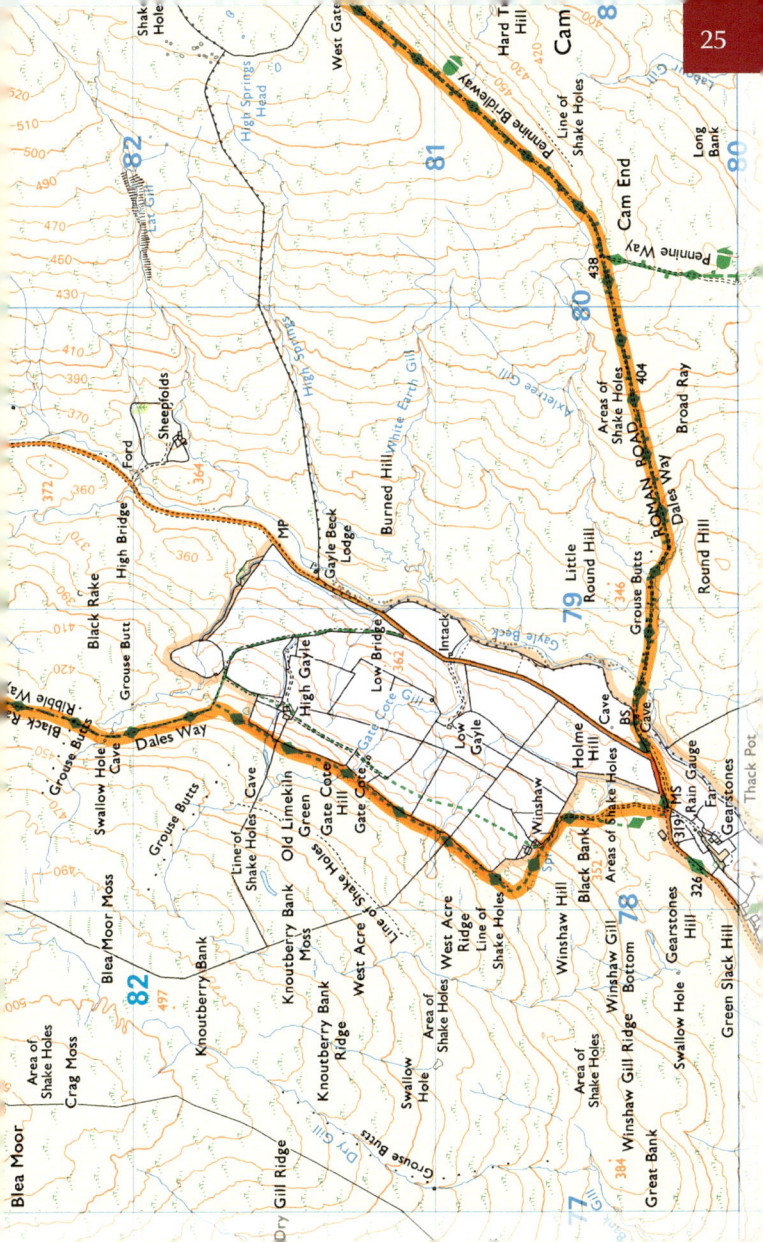

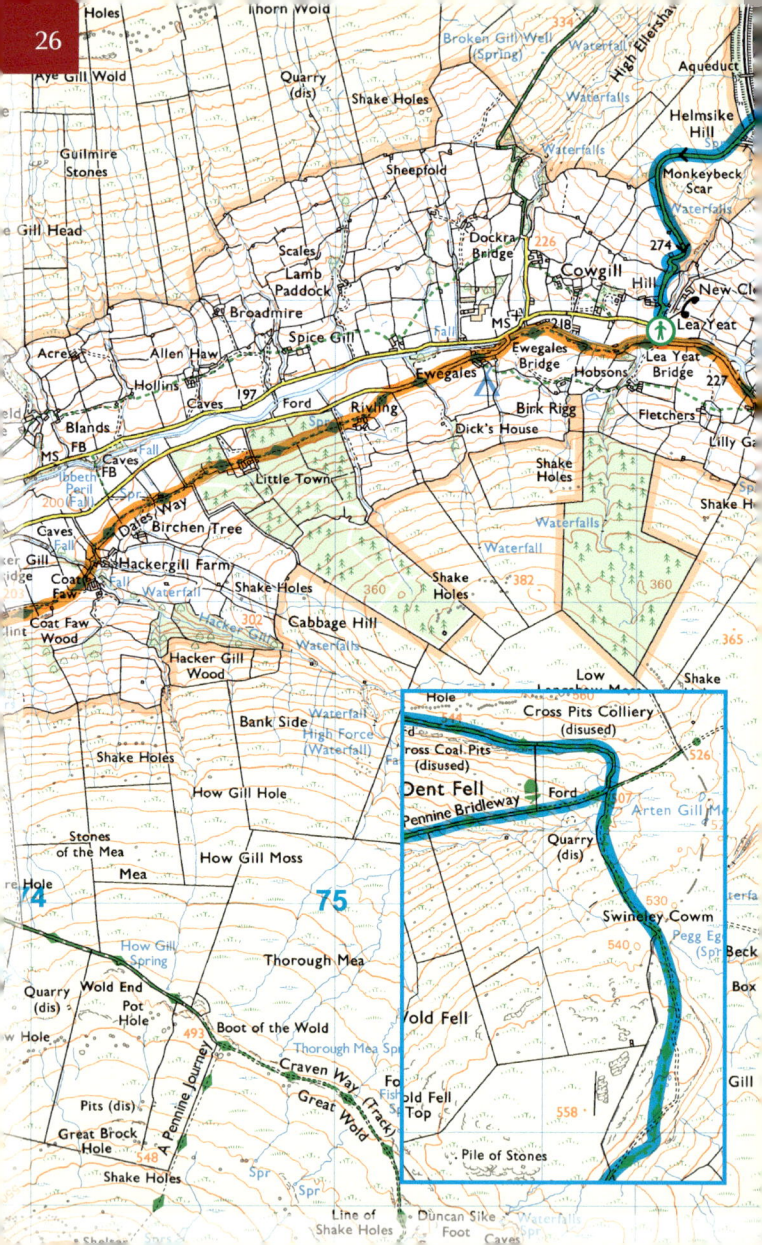

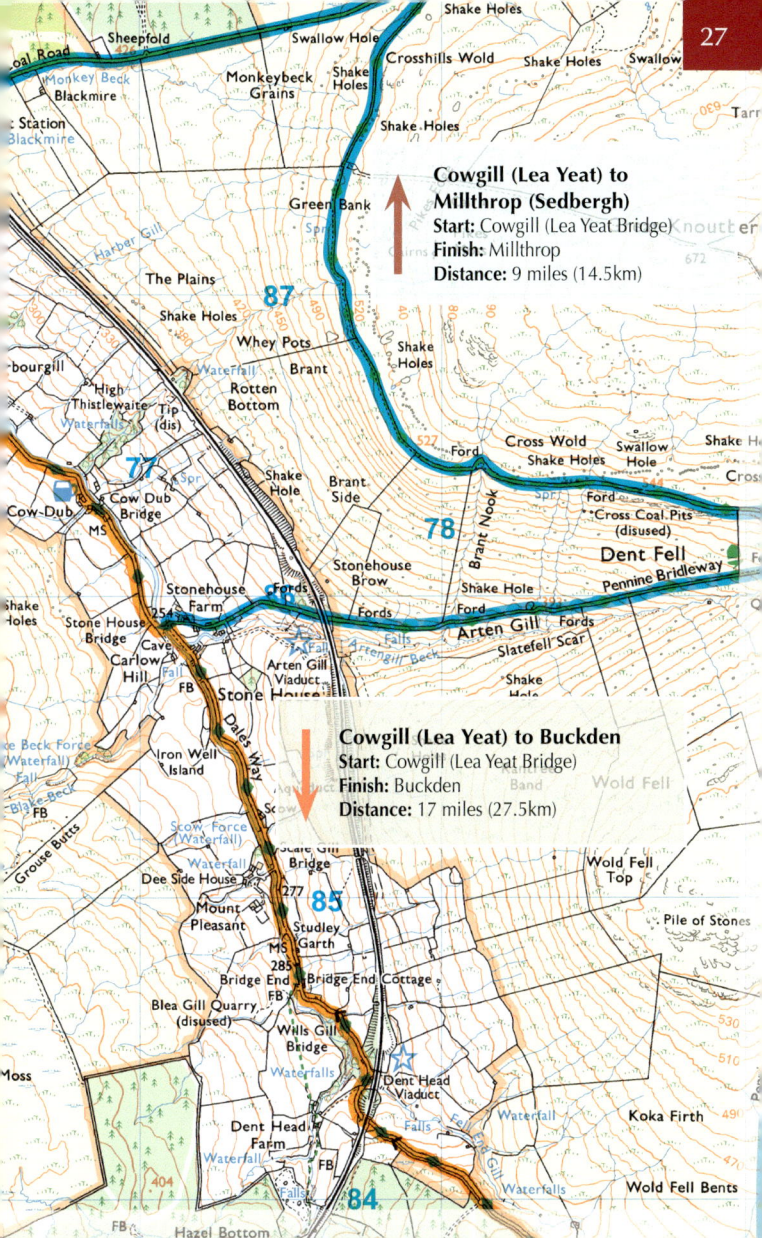

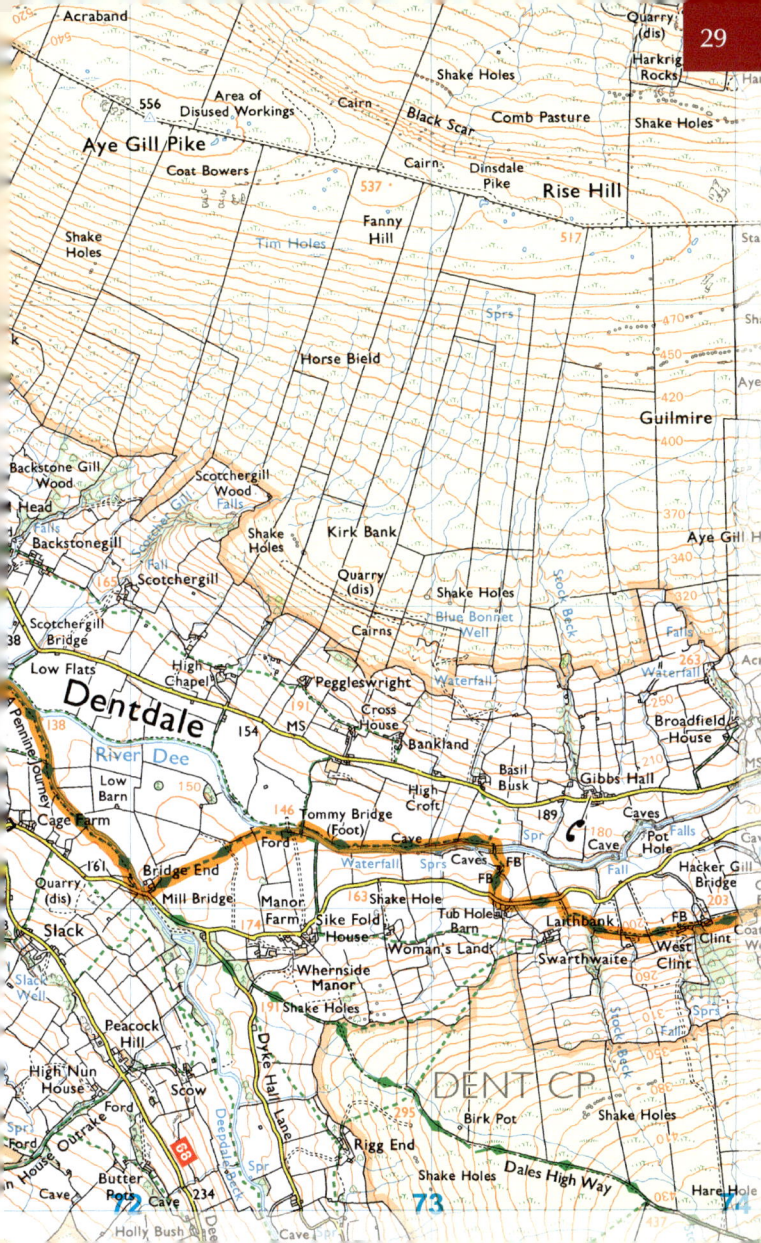

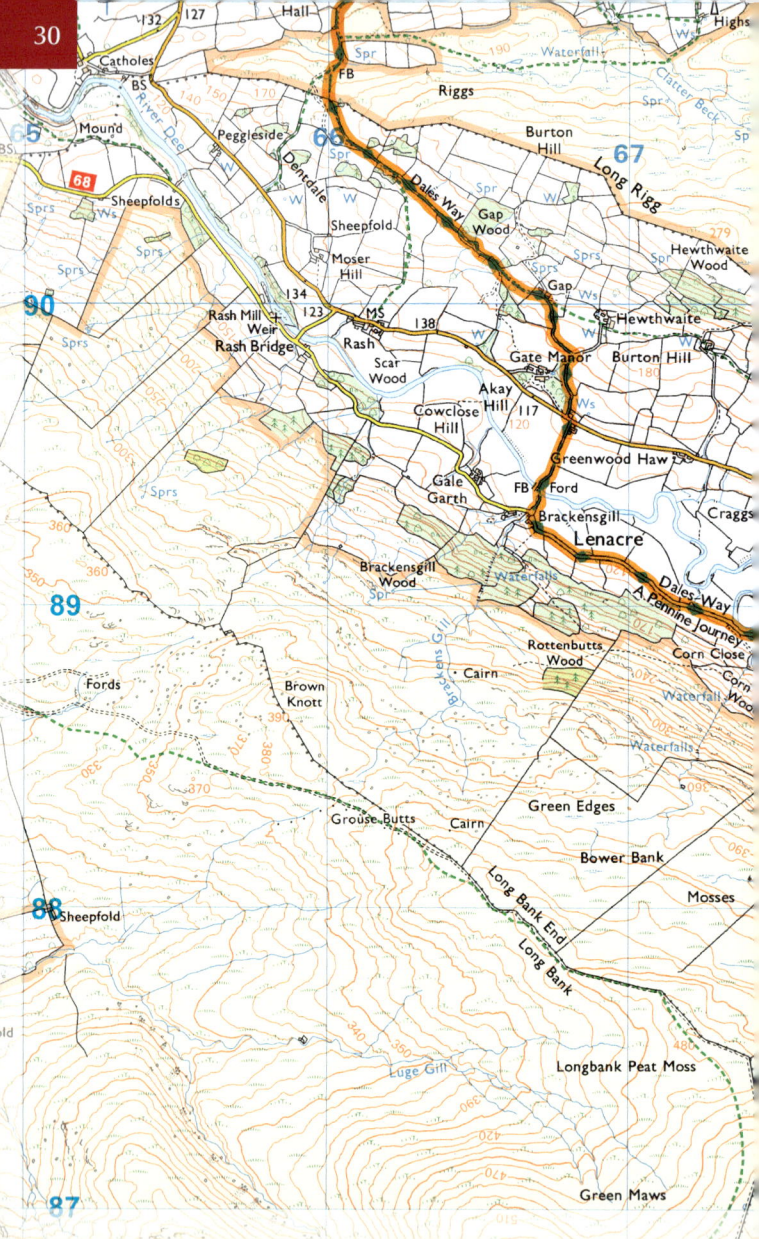

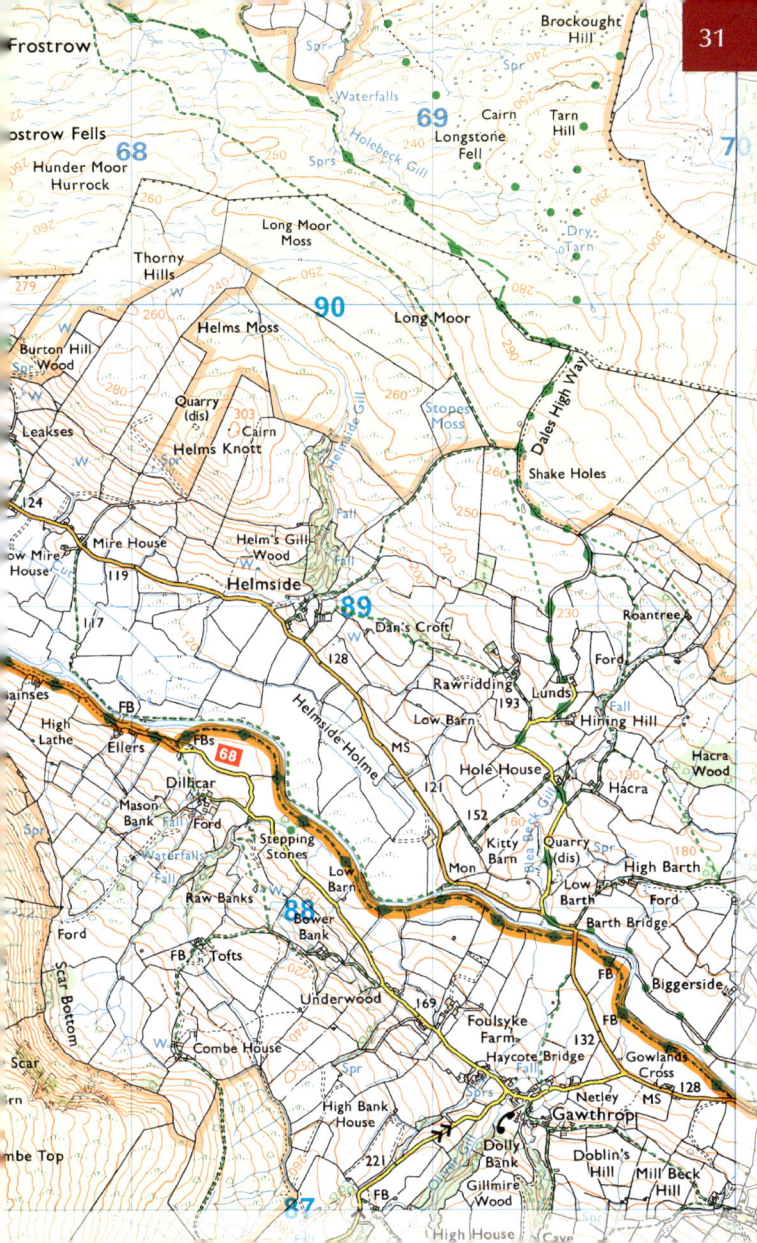

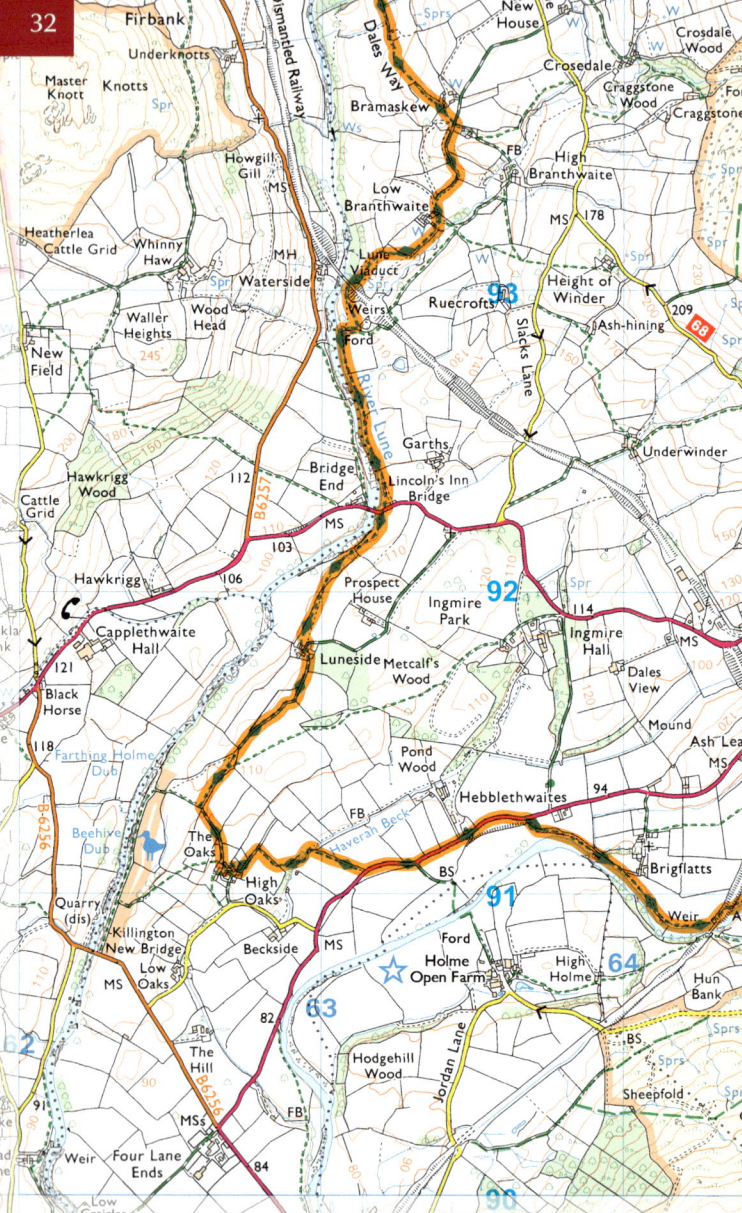

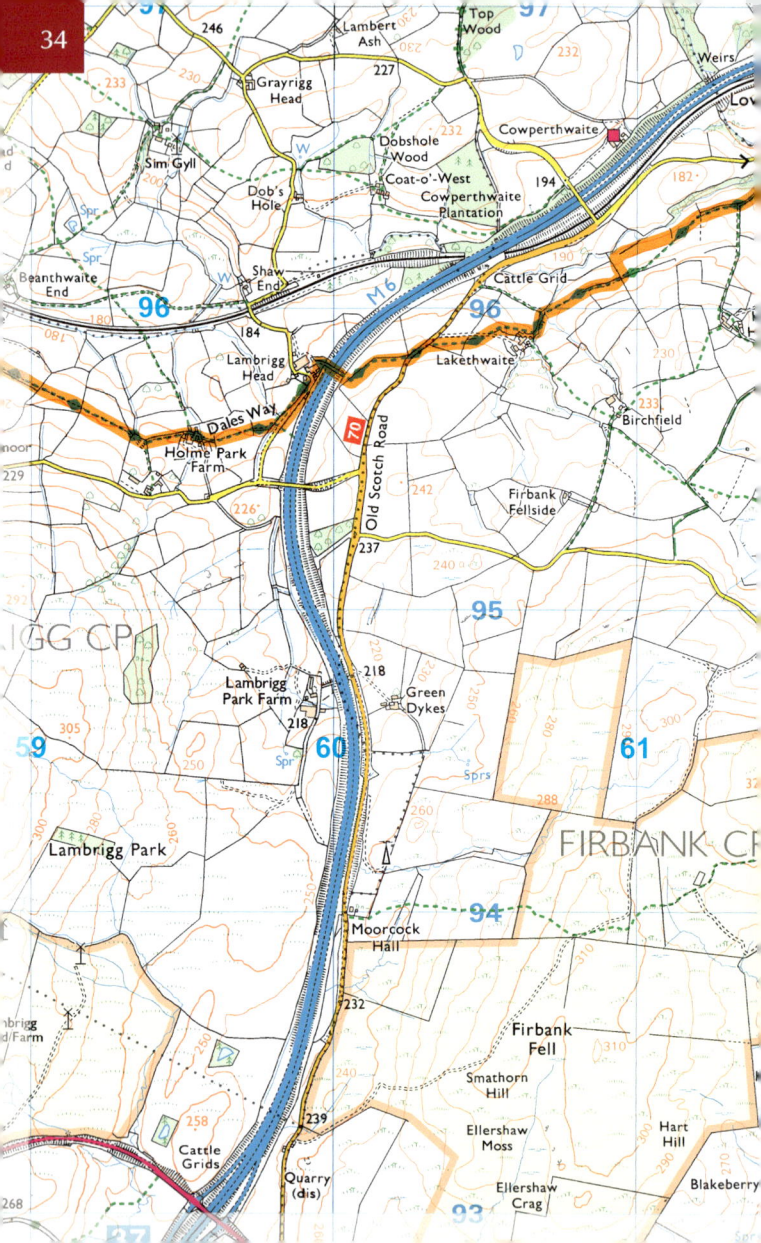

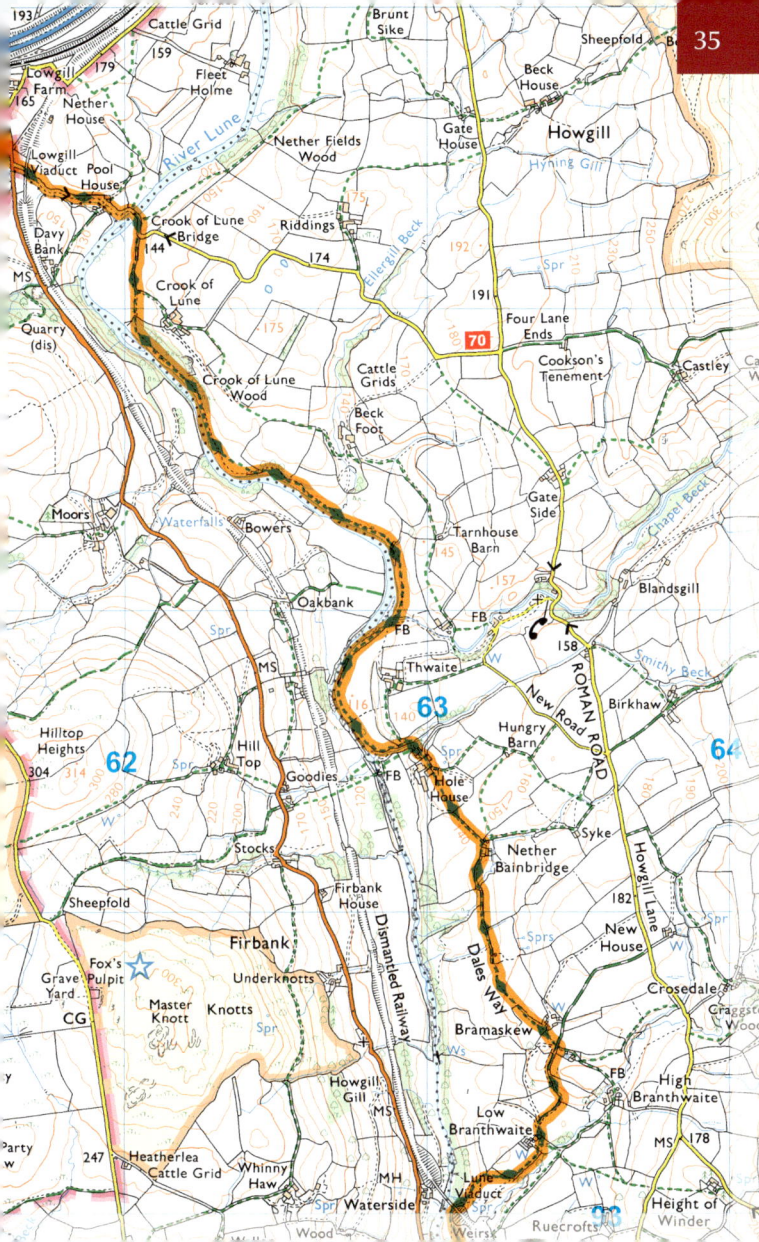

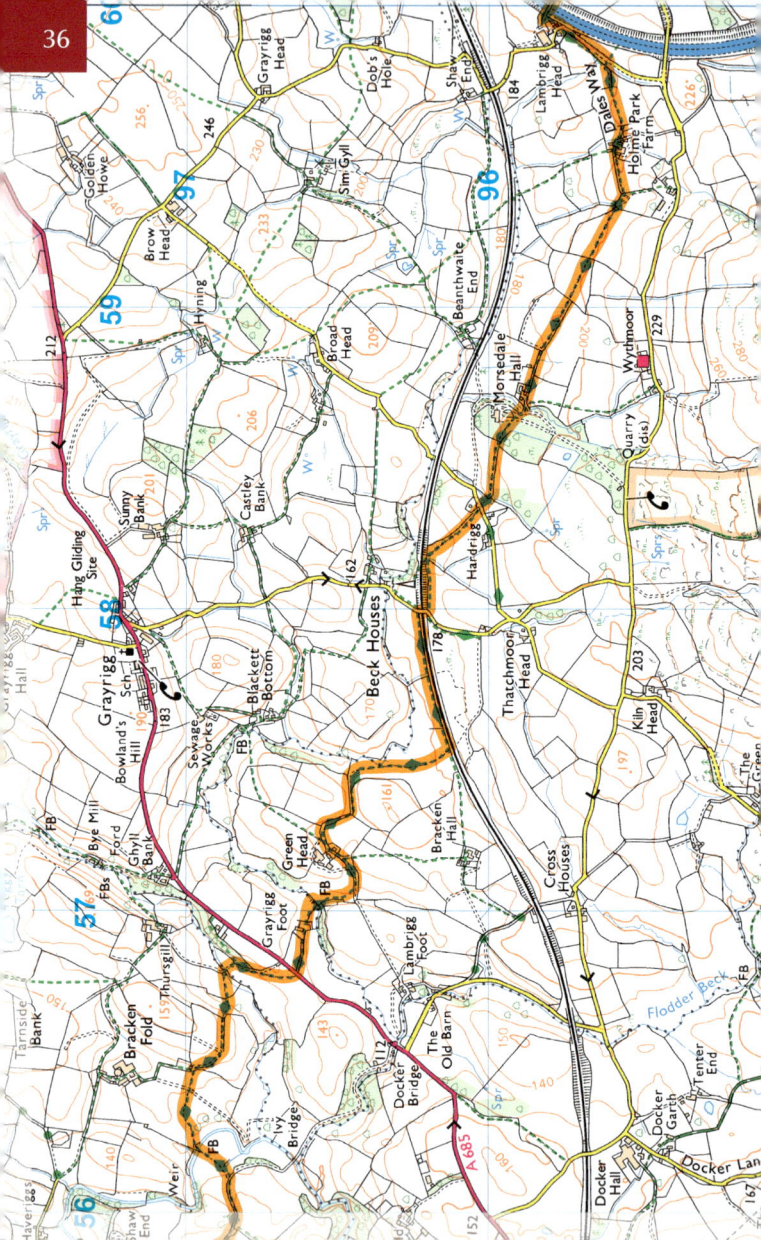

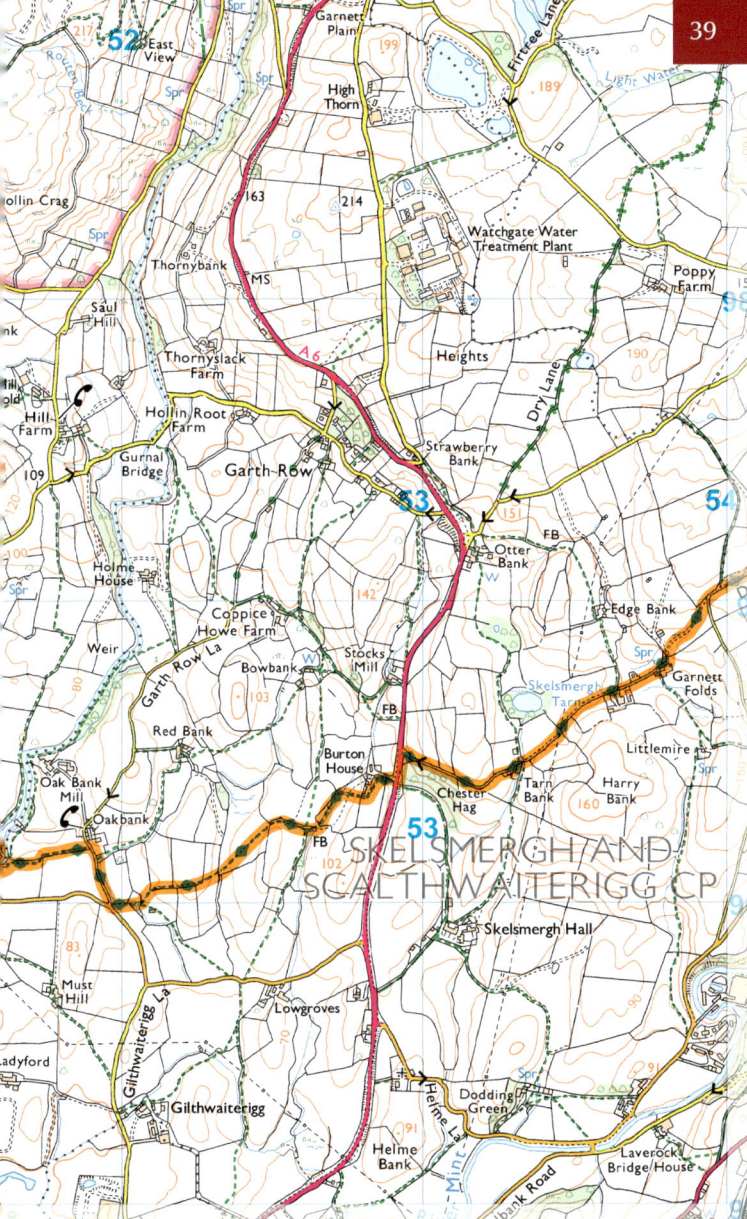

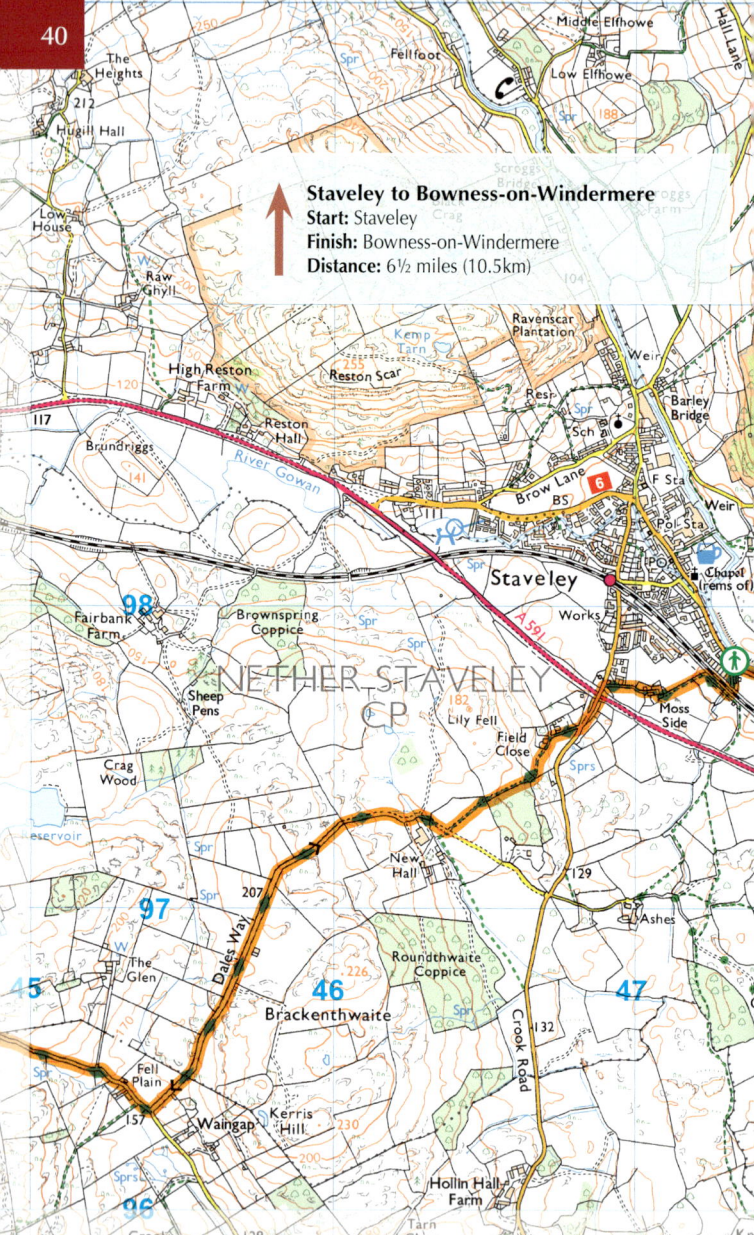

Staveley to Millthrop (Sedbergh)
Start: Staveley
Finish: Millthrop
Distance: 19 miles (31km)

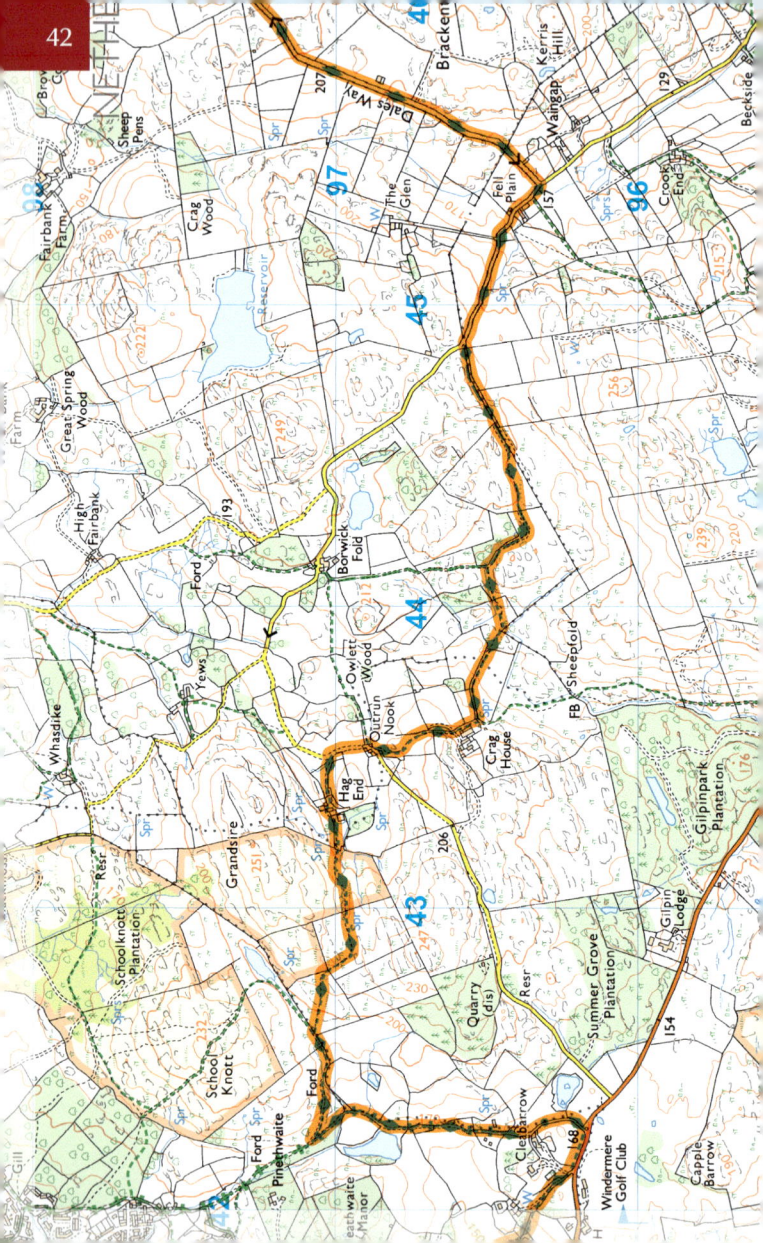

LEGEND OF SYMBOLS USED ON ORDNANCE SURVEY 1:25,000 (EXPLORER) MAPPING

ROADS AND PATHS — Not necessarily rights of way

Symbol	Description
M1 or A6(M)	Motorway
A 35	Dual carriageway
A30	Main road
B 3074	Secondary road
	Narrow road with passing places
	Road under construction
	Road generally more than 4 m wide
	Road generally less than 4 m wide
	Other road, drive or track, fenced and unfenced
	Gradient: steeper than 20% (1 in 5); 14% (1 in 7) to 20% (1 in 5)
Ferry	Ferry; Ferry P – passenger only
	Path

- S Service Area
- S Service Area
- 7 Junction Number
- T1 Toll road junction

RAILWAYS

- Multiple track / Single track — standard gauge
- Narrow gauge or Light rapid transit system (LRTS) and station
- Road over; road under; level crossing
- Cutting; tunnel; embankment
- Station, open to passengers; siding

PUBLIC RIGHTS OF WAY

- ----------- Footpath
- – – – – – Bridleway
- +++++ Byway open to all traffic
- –+–+–+– Restricted byway

The representation on this map of any other road, track or path is no evidence of the existence of a right of way

ARCHAEOLOGICAL AND HISTORICAL INFORMATION

Symbol	Description	Symbol	Description	Symbol	Description
⳾	Site of antiquity	VILLA	Roman	✱	Visible earthwork
⚔ 1066	Site of battle (with date)	Castle	Non-Roman		

Information provided by English Heritage for England and the Royal Commissions on the Ancient and Historical Monuments for Scotland and Wales

OTHER PUBLIC ACCESS

• • • Other routes with public access — The exact nature of the rights on these routes and the existence of any restrictions may be checked with the local highway authority. Alignments are based on the best information available

♦ ♦ ♦ Recreational route

♦ ♦ ♦ **National Trail** **Long Distance Route**

- - - - - Permissive footpath ⎫ Footpaths and bridleways along which landowners have permitted public use but which are not rights of way. The agreement may be withdrawn
— — — Permissive bridleway ⎭

• • • Traffic-free cycle route

1 **1** National cycle network route number – traffic free; on road

ACCESS LAND

  Firing and test ranges in the area. Danger! Observe warning notices

 Access permitted within managed controls, for example, local byelaws. Visit **www.access.mod.uk** for information

England and Wales

  Access land boundary and tint

Access land in wooded area

  Access information point

Portrayal of access land on this map is intended as a guide to land which is normally available for access on foot, for example access land created under the Countryside and Rights of Way Act 2000, and land managed by the National Trust, Forestry Commission and Woodland Trust. Access for other activities may also exist. Some restrictions will apply; some land will be excluded from open access rights. The depiction of rights of access does not imply or express any warranty as to its accuracy or completeness. Observe local signs and follow the Countryside Code.
Visit **www.countrysideaccess.gov.uk** for up-to-date information

BOUNDARIES

— + — + — National

— · — · — County (England)

— — — — Unitary Authority (UA), Metropolitan District (Met Dist), London Borough (LB) or District (Scotland & Wales are solely Unitary Authorities)

· · · · · · · · Civil Parish (CP) (England) or Community (C) (Wales)

━━━━ National Park boundary

VEGETATION

Limits of vegetation are defined by positioning of symbols

Coniferous trees

Non-coniferous trees

Coppice

Orchard

Scrub

Bracken, heath or rough grassland

Marsh, reeds or saltings

HEIGHTS AND NATURAL FEATURES

52 · Ground survey height
284 · Air survey height

Surface heights are to the nearest metre above mean sea level. Where two heights are shown, the first height is to the base of the triangulation pillar and the second (in brackets) to the highest natural point of the hill

HEIGHTS AND NATURAL FEATURES (continued)

Vertical face/cliff

Loose rock · Boulders · Outcrop · Scree

Contours are at 5 or 10 metre vertical intervals

Water	
Mud	
Sand; sand and shingle	

SELECTED TOURIST AND LEISURE INFORMATION

Symbol	Description	Symbol	Description
	Building of historic interest		Nature reserve
	Cadw		National Trust
	Heritage centre		Other tourist feature
	Camp site	P	Parking
	Caravan site	P&R	Park and ride, all year
	Camping and caravan site	P&R	Park and ride, seasonal
	Castle / fort		Picnic site
	Cathedral / Abbey		Preserved railway
	Craft centre	PC	Public Convenience
	Country park		Public house/s
	Cycle trail		Recreation / leisure / sports centre
	Mountain bike trail		Roman site (Hadrian's Wall only)
	Cycle hire		Slipway
	English Heritage		Telephone, emergency
	Fishing		Telephone, public
	Forestry Commission Visitor centre		Telephone, roadside assistance
	Garden / arboretum		Theme / pleasure park
	Golf course or links		Viewpoint
	Historic Scotland	V	Visitor centre
i	Information centre, all year		Walks / trails
i	Information centre, seasonal		World Heritage site / area
	Horse riding		Water activites
	Museum		Boat trips
	National Park Visitor Centre (park logo) e.g. Yorkshire Dales		Boat hire

(For complete legend and symbols, see any OS Explorer map)

THE DALES WAY

This map booklet accompanies the latest edition of Terry Marsh's guidebook to the Dales Way, described principally in a northbound direction (with summary route description southbound), between Ilkley and Bowness-on-Windermere. The guidebook features 1:100,000 mapping alongside detailed step-by-step route description, with lots of planning advice and information about local history, geography and wildlife. The guide also includes a variant watershed crossing between Cam Houses and Dentdale.

Streamside strolling, not far from Ilkley (Stage 1)

OTHER CICERONE TRAIL GUIDES

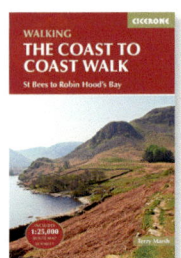 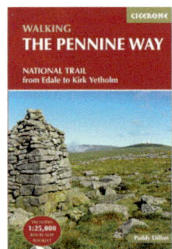 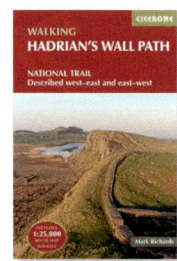

Cicerone Trail Guides
The South West Coast Path
The South Downs Way
The North Downs Way
The Ridgeway National Trail
The Thames Path
The Cotswold Way
The Peddars Way and
    Norfolk Coast Path
The Cleveland Way and
    the Yorkshire Wolds Way
Cycling the Pennine Bridleway
The Pennine Way
Hadrian's Wall Path
The Pembrokeshire Coast Path
Offa's Dyke Path
Glyndŵr's Way
The Southern Upland Way
The Speyside Way
The West Highland Way
The Great Glen Way

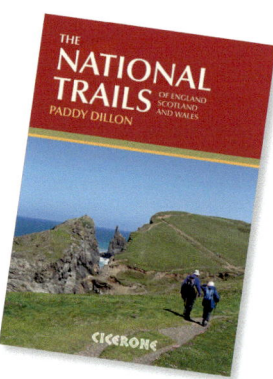

Visit our website for a full
list of Cicerone Trail Guides
www.cicerone.co.uk